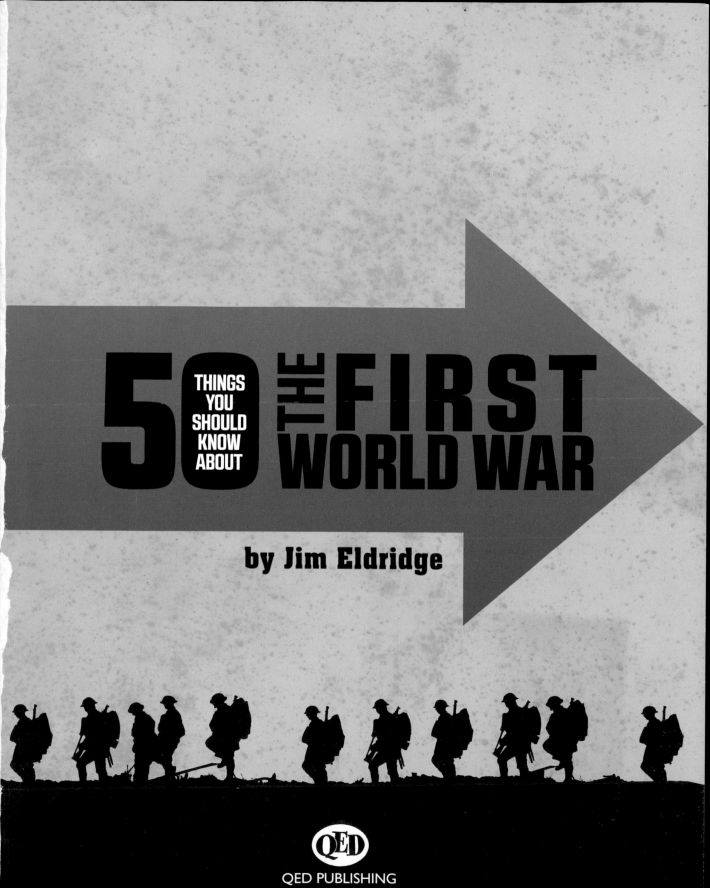

50
THINGS YOU SHOULD KNOW ABOUT

THE FIRST WORLD WAR

by Jim Eldridge

QED PUBLISHING

Consultant: Professor Ian Beckett,
Professor of Military History,
Rutherford College, University of Kent
Editor: Ruth Symons
Designers: Angela Ball and Dave Ball
Editorial Director: Victoria Garrard
Art Director: Laura Roberts-Jensen

Copyright © QED Publishing 2014

First published in the UK in 2014 by
QED Publishing
A Quarto Group company
The Old Brewery, 6 Blundell Street,
London, N7 9BH

www.qed-publishing.co.uk

A catalogue record for this book is available from
the British Library.

ISBN 978 1 78171 589 5

Printed in China

Words in bold are explained
in the Glossary on page 78.

CONTENTS

INTRODUCTION

For hundreds of years, countries in Europe had been at war with one another. Each nation wanted more power and more land, which they hoped to take from the countries around them. By the start of the 20th century, most European nations ruled a handful of other countries, known as an empire.

THE FRANCO-PRUSSIAN WAR

Before 1871, Germany was a group of small kingdoms. The biggest of these was Prussia. In 1870, Prussia went to war with France. When Prussia won in 1871, it seized French land and joined with other kingdoms to form the nation of Germany. The conflict left people in France hungry for revenge and determined to win back their land.

STICKING TOGETHER

After the Franco-Prussian War, France worried about another attack, and Russia was suspicious of Germany's plans to expand. France and Russia agreed they would come to each other's aid if Germany ever attacked. At the same time, France and England made an agreement which later became an **alliance** against Germany.

▼ The Franco-Prussian War (1870-1871) created many tensions between France and Germany.

BALKAN WARS

In 1912, Montenegro, Serbia, Greece and Bulgaria fought the Ottoman (Turkish) Empire. Then, in 1914, Bulgaria turned on its allies, starting a second war. Bulgaria lost lots of land, while Serbia nearly doubled in size. Serbia's size frightened many countries. It looked like another war might be just around the corner...

▼ The Turkish army waiting for action in Greece, 1912.

King George V of Britain

Kaiser Wilhelm II of Germany

Alexandra, wife of Tsar Nicholas II of Russia

THE ARMS RACE

European nations feared that their rivals might try to seize land from them, so they did their best to defend themselves: they built bigger and better armies, with the latest, most powerful weapons. Germany was particularly jealous of Britain's navy. Between 1906 and 1914, Germany built 20 new battleships!

1914

The year war began

When the heir to the Austro-Hungarian throne was killed in 1914, it was just months before all of Europe was at war. Armies marched away, expecting a quick, glorious victory. Both sides were sure the war would be over by Christmas. No one was ready for the long, drawn-out struggle that was to come…

▼ *Men in England leaving their homes to join the armed forces in 1914.*

UNITED KINGDOM

North Sea

London ★

English Channel

NETHER-LANDS

Brussels ★ **2** BELGIUM

Paris ★ **4** LUX.

FRANCE

SWITZ-ERLAND

PORTUGAL

SPAIN

Corsica (France)

Balearic Is. (Spain)

Sardinia (Italy)

Mediterranean Sea

ALGERIA

TUNISIA

KEY EVENTS

28 JUNE
Archduke Ferdinand is assassinated (see page 8).

28 JULY
Austria-Hungary declares war on Serbia. Russia sends troops to defend Serbia.

1 AUGUST
Germany declares war on Russia.

3 AUGUST
Germany declares war on France.

3 AUGUST
Germany invades Belgium. Britain declares war on Germany (see page 9).

NORWAY

SWEDEN

FINLAND

DENMARK

Baltic Sea

Latvia

Lithuania

Berlin ★

GERMANY

Poland

RUSSIA

Ukraine

Vienna ★

AUSTRIA-HUNGARY

ROMANIA

Adriatic Sea

MONTE-NEGRO

SERBIA

BULGARIA

Black Sea

ITALY

ALBANIA

GREECE

Constantinople ★

Aegean Sea

TURKEY

Sicily (Italy)

ALLIES VS CENTRAL POWERS

At the start of the war the two sides were:

✹ **THE ALLIES:** the French Republic and Empire, the British Empire, the Russian Empire, Belgium, Serbia and Montenegro

✹ **THE CENTRAL POWERS:** the German Empire, the Austro-Hungarian Empire and the Ottoman (Turkish) Empire

KEY

▮ CENTRAL POWERS (August 1914)

▮ ALLIES (August 1914)

▮ NEUTRAL NATIONS

▬ Front lines at the end of 1914

✺1 Archduke Franz Ferdinand assassinated (see page 8)

✺2 Battle of Mons (see page 10)

✺3 Battle of Tannenberg (see page 11)

✺4 Battle of the Marne (see page 12)

0 ———— 300 miles

0 ———— 500 kilometres

AUGUST
War spreads to Africa (see page 22).

23 AUGUST
The Battle of Mons (see page 10).

27–30 AUGUST
The Battle of Tannenberg (see page 11).

5–9 SEPTEMBER
The Battle of the Marne (see page 12).

SEPTEMBER
The first trenches are dug on the Western Front (see page 14).

7

The assassination of Franz Ferdinand

On 28 June 1914, Archduke Franz Ferdinand, heir to the Austro-Hungarian throne, visited Sarajevo in Bosnia. There, he and his wife were shot and killed by Gavrilo Princip, who was part of a Serbian terrorist group. The **assassination** was the spark that led to war.

DEFENCE TREATIES

Several European countries were bound to each other by defence **treaties**. These promised that the countries involved would support each other in the event of war.

Germany, Austria-Hungary and Italy signed the Triple Alliance in 1882.

Russia, France and Britain formed an alliance called the Triple Entente in 1907.

▶ Archduke Franz Ferdinand

CHOOSING SIDES

Austria-Hungary declared war on Serbia. Germany backed its ally Austria-Hungary, while Russia supported Serbia. When Germany declared war against Russia, the French took up arms against Germany.

Just two months after the assassination, 14 countries had joined the war.

The Schlieffen Plan

Germany had been preparing for war for years. In 1905, Count Alfred von Schlieffen made plans to attack the countries he saw as Germany's biggest enemies: France and Russia. He planned to defeat France, then turn on Russia. By 1914, Germany had an army of over 4 million – it was ready to put its plan into action.

ASSUMPTIONS OF THE PLAN

The German army assumed that things would go to plan. But when they marched into Belgium on 3 August 1914, their assumptions did not match up to reality.

ASSUMPTIONS

1. Belgium would be easily beaten.

2. Britain would stay out of the conflict.

3. Russia would take six weeks to mobilise its army (move it to the action).

REALITY

1. The Belgian army put up strong resistance. They delayed the German attack on France by a month.

2. Britain declared war on Germany on 4 August.

3. Russia mobilised its army in just 10 days.

A WAR ON TWO FRONTS

By the time German troops reached the French border, the French army was waiting for them. Meanwhile, the Russian army was approaching from the East. Germany was now fighting a war on two **fronts**: the Western Front (against France and Belgium) and the Eastern Front (against Russia).

THE WESTERN FRONT

GERMANY

THE EASTERN FRONT

FRANCE

AUSTRIA-HUNGARY

ITALY

◄ *This map shows the Eastern Front and the Western Front as red lines.*

The cavalry

4

When the war broke out, all armies still had a cavalry: a force of soldiers riding on horseback. The British army alone owned **25,000 horses**, but only **80 motor vehicles**.

▼ The British cavalry charge at German forces during the retreat from the Battle of Mons.

THE BATTLE OF MONS

In August, the British landed in France and marched to face the German army at Mons, in Belgium. Nearby, two British cavalry regiments attacked the German army at Élouges. They were armed with swords, lances and revolvers, but came up against machine guns. 250 British soldiers and 300 horses died in the attack.

STANDARD BRITISH REVOLVER (WEBLEY)
Speed: *20–30 shots per minute*
Range: *45 metres*

STANDARD GERMAN MACHINE GUN (MASCHINENGEWEHR 08)
Speed: *4000 shots per minute*
Range: *2000–3500 metres*

A HORSE'S WORK

After August 1914, cavalry charges were reduced on the Western Front. Horses were put to work pulling **artillery**, ambulances and supply wagons. They were more reliable than motor vehicles and better at getting through deep mud.

The Battle of Tannenberg

On 7 August, two Russian armies invaded Germany. Then, on 27 August, the German army faced them at the Battle of Tannenberg. It was the first big battle on the Eastern Front.

▼ German soldiers duck as a shell explodes during the battle.

RUSSIAN ARMY vs GERMAN ARMY

✹ 1.5 million soldiers (from a population of 167 million)	✹ 4 million soldiers (from a population of 65 million)
✹ 2 machine guns per battalion (1000 men)	✹ 36 machine guns per battalion (1000 men)
✹ Shortage of trained officers	✹ Educated, well-trained officers
✹ Messages sent over open radio lines	✹ Coded radio transmissions

▼ Thousands of Russians were taken prisoner after the battle. Here they are queueing for food in a prison camp.

WHAT HAPPENED?

The two Russian armies did not communicate with each other, and their plans quickly fell apart. 150,000 Russians went into the battle, but only 10,000 escaped. The rest were killed, wounded or taken prisoner. This early victory gave the Germans hope that the war would soon be won!

The Russian commanders had fallen out in 1905 and vowed never to talk to each other again!

The Battle of the Marne

In August 1914, the German army headed for Paris. The Allies had been retreating, but they stood their ground at the Marne River, east of Paris. The German army advanced quickly. By early September, they were just 50 km from the edge of the city.

WHAT HAPPENED?

A combined force of French and British Expeditionary Force (BEF) troops stopped the German advance. In mid-September they launched a counter-attack, which forced the German army back.

◀ *German soldiers manning machine guns at the Battle of the Marne.*

Parks in Paris were filled with cattle so the city would not starve.

▼ *French taxis line up on the streets of Paris.*

TAXI!

On 6 September, Paris seemed to be just hours away from invasion. Reinforcements were summoned but they couldn't be moved to the front. Then a French general called Gallieni had a brilliant idea. He ordered every taxi in the city to collect soldiers and drive them to the Marne. Around 600 taxis carried 6000 reserve troops to the front.

YPRES

The fighting on the Western Front centred around the town of Ypres in the Flanders area of Belgium. The British took control of Ypres, and held it throughout the war, despite constant and heavy attacks by German forces. Most British soldiers couldn't say the word Ypres, so they called it 'Wipers'.

The race to the sea

Both sides tried to sneak behind the enemy's lines by going north around the edge of the fighting. As the armies crept further and further north, they built trenches along the way. This became known as 'The Race to the Sea'.

5 BIG BATTLES

There were five battles at Ypres during the war:

1 **First Battle of Ypres**
(October 19–November 22, 1914)

2 **Second Battle of Ypres**
(April 22–May 15, 1915)

3 **Third Battle of Ypres**
(July 31–November 6, 1917)
also known as Passchendaele

4 **Fourth Battle of Ypres**
(April 9–April 29, 1918)
also known as the Battle of the Lys

5 **Fifth Battle of Ypres**
(September 28–October 2, 1918)

▼ Before the war, Ypres was a wealthy city. This photograph shows its famous Cloth Hall before it was destroyed.

▼ By the end of the war, Ypres had been destroyed by shellfire and bombing raids.

The trenches

THE FRONT LINE

The trench nearest the enemy was known as the front line. This was where most fighting took place: soldiers shot at the enemy, and sometimes climbed out of the trench to attack them.

Other trenches linked together behind the front line. They held kitchens, first aid points and equipment.

Along the Western Front, both sides dug trenches, where their troops could shelter from attack. These were ditches, deep enough to protect soldiers from bullets and flying **shrapnel**. Most were basic structures, with just wooden planks and sandbags to support them. As the war continued, the Germans used concrete to reinforce their shelters.

▶ *A British soldier manning a captured German trench on the Western Front.*

1 Firestep: a ledge so soldiers could look over the top of the trench

2 Duckboards: planks laid over mud and floodwater

3 Dugout: a small hole in the earth where soldiers could sleep

4 Parapet: the front of the trench, made from sandbags or earth

▲ *This diagram shows the layout of a typical trench.*

The front line was built in a zigzag shape. If a **shell** exploded inside a trench, its twists and turns would help contain the blast. And if the enemy took the trench, the zigzag shape would slow them down.

▲ This is a typical example of a zigzag shaped trench.

32,200 km of trenches had been dug by the end of the war! Stretched out end-to-end they would nearly wrap around the world.

NO MAN'S LAND

The area between the two front lines was known as 'no man's land' because it didn't belong to either side. It was lined with rows of barbed wire, to slow down attacks by the enemy. It was often full of dead and dying soldiers.

▼ Flares were thrown into no man's land to light it up. They could expose enemy soldiers trying to attack under cover of darkness.

The colonies

Many European countries had overseas **colonies**, which were part of their vast empires. When war was declared in 1914, many colonies sent troops to Europe to help in the war.

INDIAN REGIMENTS

Over 1.5 million Indians fought alongside the British Empire. Indian troops wore similar uniforms to the British, but Sikh soldiers wore turbans instead of steel helmets. Some Indian soldiers rode into battle on camels. In 1915, there was a camel cavalry charge near the Suez Canal!

▶ *Members of an Indian cavalry regiment stop to consult a map.*

COLONIAL TROOPS

By 1915, the British needed more soldiers – so they called on soldiers from their colonies in the West Indies. In a similar move, the French raised troops from their colonies in Africa and Southeast Asia. By supporting the Allies, the colonies hoped they would be given more freedom and opportunities after the war.

▲ *These Senegalese soldiers went to the Western Front to support French troops.*

The Ottoman Empire

By 1914, the Ottoman (Turkish) Empire was nearly 600 years old. It had lost much of its territory in the Balkan Wars (see page 5) and hoped to win it back by siding with the Central Powers. So, in August 1914, Turkey signed a secret agreement with Germany.

THE IMPORTANCE OF OIL

The Allies and the Central Powers both needed oil for their vehicles, ships and aeroplanes. Most oil came from the Middle East, in land ruled by the Ottoman Empire. Both sides were worried about protecting their oil supplies, so they decided to send troops into the Middle East.

SENDING IN THE TROOPS

In November, a force of British and Indian soldiers arrived in the Middle East to protect Allied oil supplies. After a short battle with the Turkish, they seized the port of Basra, which they held until the end of the war. However, fighting continued across the Middle East until 1918.

▼ Turkish troops gathering in the streets in 1914.

England under attack

Civilians away from the fronts thought that they were safe from the war. But on 16 December 1914, the German navy attacked the towns of Scarborough, Hartlepool and Whitby on the east coast of England. Factories, railways, churches and houses were all destroyed. Nearly 600 people were injured and 137 were killed.

▼ *Damage in Hartlepool after the attack.*

ZEPPELINS

Later in the war, zeppelins were used to drop bombs on towns, or targets such as factories. Zeppelins were airships filled with hydrogen gas. They were often shot down by bullets designed to set their hydrogen gas on fire.

▼ *This is the German zeppelin L3, which was used in later bombing raids on Britain.*

A Christmas truce

On Christmas Day 1914, there was an unofficial **ceasefire** along parts of the Western Front. Soldiers crossed no man's land to sing carols, play football and swap gifts of food, buttons and tobacco. One soldier even gave people free haircuts!

▼ *German and Allied troops come together on Christmas Day, 1914.*

CHRISTMAS GIFTS

The German government sent their soldiers Christmas trees, which they strung with candles and put up in the trenches. Meanwhile, in Britain Princess Mary organized tins of chocolates and cigarettes to be sent to soldiers.

▼ *Soldiers from opposing sides pose for a photograph together on Christmas Day, 1914.*

NEVER AGAIN

The truce was a brief break from the horrors of fighting. But the generals on each side were furious when they heard what had happened. It was the first and last truce of the war.

(13) 1915

The war spreads

On the Western Front, neither side was making any gains – weeks of fighting could result in just a few kilometres of gained land. However, new weapons were being developed, including deadly poison gases. Meanwhile, more and more countries became involved in the war and thousands of men went to fight.

UNITED KINGDOM

North Sea

London ★

NETHER-LANDS

English Channel

Brussels ★

BELGIUM

LUX.

Paris ★

FRANCE

SWITZ-ERLAND

PORTUGAL

SPAIN

Corsica (France)

Balearic Is. (Spain)

Sardinia (Italy)

Mediterranean Sea

ALGERIA

TUNISIA

▼ *Allied soldiers wearing gas masks during a training exercise.*

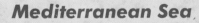

KEY EVENTS

JANUARY
Poison gas is first used
(see page 25).

JANUARY–JUNE
Allied campaign in Cameroon in Africa.

25 APRIL
Allied landings on Gallipoli in Turkey
(see page 27).

7 MAY
Sinking of the Lusitania by a German U-boat
(see page 29).

NORWAY

SWEDEN

FINLAND

DENMARK

Baltic Sea

Latvia

Lithuania

RUSSIA

Berlin
★

GERMANY

③ ★ Warsaw
Poland

U k r a i n e

Vienna
★

**AUSTRIA-
HUNGARY**

ROMANIA

Black Sea

ITALY

SERBIA

MONTE-
NEGRO

ALBANIA

BULGARIA

GREECE

Constantinople
★

TURKEY

*Aegean
Sea*

①

Sicily
(Italy)

KEY

CENTRAL POWERS
(August 1915)

ALLIES
(August 1915)

NEUTRAL NATIONS

Front lines at the
end of 1915

① Gallipoli landings
(see page 27)

② Sinking of the Lusitania
(see page 29)

③ Germans capture Warsaw
(4th August 1915)

0 _____ 300 miles

0 _____ 500 kilometres

23 MAY
Italy joins the war
(see page 41).

4 AUGUST
Germans capture
Warsaw in Poland.

WINTER 1915
The Western Front
remains the same.

The war in Africa

Several European countries had colonies in Africa: some were ruled by the Allies; others by Germany. In late 1914, the African colonies went to war with each other. The fighting was no longer contained to Europe.

THE BIG PICTURE
Over time, many German colonies surrendered to the Allies – Togoland surrendered in 1914; Southwest Africa in 1915 and Cameroon in 1916. However, German forces kept fighting along the Mozambique border until 1918.

▲ Soldiers of the German colonial army assemble in German Southwest Africa.

Mediterranean Sea

Suez Canal

EGYPT

Red Sea

THE SUEZ CANAL
The Suez Canal in Egypt linked the Red Sea to the Mediterranean. It was an important short cut for ships that wished to avoid sailing right around Africa. The Suez Canal was under British protection, which gave the Allies a big advantage during the war. In February 1915, British forces fought off a German-Ottoman attack on the canal.

Railways

GAUGES

The railways in different countries used different gauges – the distance between rails on the track. This caused problems when armies crossed from one country to another. Often troops and supplies had to be unloaded and put on different trains every time they crossed a border!

Railways were the quickest and cheapest way of moving troops and supplies around. A smooth-running line could make the difference between winning a battle and losing it. Because of their importance, railway lines and trains became the target of attacks, both by land and by air.

▼ Railways were used to transport the very heaviest guns to and from the front.

One German general said: "Build no more fortresses. Build railways."

TRENCH RAILWAYS

Small, portable railways were used to move food and soldiers to the front line trenches. The tracks came in five-metre sections, which could be easily moved and put into place.

▶ Men assemble a railway behind the front line on the Western Front.

Life in the trenches

Life in the trenches was muddy, miserable and dangerous. Soldiers took turns to be on sentry duty, watching the enemy line. Other duties included repairing the trenches, filling sandbags and cleaning weapons.

▼ Trenches often flooded. Even when the water was pumped out, it could be impossible for soldiers to keep their feet dry.

DISEASES

Standing in muddy, flooded trenches gave many soldiers 'trench foot' – a disease that made their feet swell up painfully. Soldiers on both sides were prone to catching lice. They also caught diseases from the trench rats!

ON PATROL

The most dangerous duty was patrolling no man's land. Patrols had to creep out at night to repair communication lines, search for survivors or spy on the enemy.

OVER THE TOP

Now and then each side sent soldiers into the enemy's trenches, to gather information or catch prisoners. Soldiers had to climb out of the trenches and march across no man's land, while under attack from shells, machine-gun fire and **snipers**.

Poison gas

Poison gas was first used in January 1915, when the Germans fired it at the Russians. On this occasion, cold weather made the gas freeze and sink harmlessly to the ground. Windy weather could also be a problem. The first British gas attack failed when the wind changed, and blew the gas back towards the British!

Poison gas was a new weapon, designed to kill or injure the enemy. There were several types of gas: tear gas made the eyes water; chlorine and phosgene attacked the lungs and led to drowning; mustard gas burned the body inside and out.

GAS MASKS

The earliest gas masks were made from a pad of cotton soaked in water or soda. Some soldiers made their own gas masks from handkerchiefs, towels or bandages soaked in urine! Later in the war, soldiers were provided with specially made gas masks.

◄ A German gas mask used between 1915 and 1918.

▼ These were the first basic gas masks issued to British soldiers in 1915.

Guns and artillery

Artillery, or heavy field guns, fired large explosives called shells from behind the trenches. Artillery guns took up to 12 men to work them. One shell could weigh up to 900 kg! The very biggest guns were mounted on railway trucks.

◄ A field gun behind British lines.

A German gun called the 'Kaiser Wilhelm' could fire a 120 kg shell up to 130 km!

MACHINE GUNS

Machine guns had to be positioned on a flat surface and manned by four to six men. A machine gun could fire over 400 shots a minute.

▶ A German machine gun from 1916.

RIFLES

Most soldiers were issued with rifles. These could fire around 15 shots a minute. Many had a small, sword-like weapon at the end, called a bayonet. Bayonets could be used for close-quarter fighting inside the trenches.

▲ A British rifle used in the First World War.

The Gallipoli Campaign

TURKEY

Gallipoli Peninsula

Constantinople

Sea of Marmara

TURKEY

The Allies thought they could win if they could capture Turkey and cut off Germany's oil supplies. In April 1915, they sent battle-ships towards Turkey's capital, Constantinople. But there were mines underwater, and the ships faced heavy gunfire. The allies had to attack over land or else give up.

GALLIPOLI LANDINGS

On 25 April 1915, troops from Australia, New Zealand, Britain and France landed along the Gallipoli Peninsula. They faced heavy fire from the minute they stepped off their ships.

DIGGING IN

The Allied forces couldn't move forwards, so they dug trenches along the beaches. After nine months of trench warfare, through a baking summer and a freezing winter, the Allies finally retreated.

480,000 Allied troops took part in the campaign. Over 200,000 of them were killed or wounded.

▼ Australian forces in Anzac Cove on the Gallipoli Peninsula in September 1915.

The war at sea

At the start of the war, Britain's navy was the biggest in the world. It formed a **blockade** to stop boats going to or from Germany. By 1915, this had created food shortages in Germany. The German navy fought back using U-boats: submarines which fired **torpedoes** at British navy ships. Over time, the U-boats started attacking other ships too!

U-BOATS

U-boat stands for 'Unterseeboot', meaning submarine boat. Conditions on U-boats were hot and crowded, and could be perilous.

▲ Two sailors in the engine room of a German U-boat. There was little room to move about on-board submarines.

SINKING OF THE LUSITANIA

Ships that weren't in the navy were supposed to be safe from U-boats. But on 7 May 1915, a British passenger liner called the *Lusitania* was hit by two German torpedoes. The ship sank, killing 1198 people, including 124 Americans. This event angered the American public and made some of them think about joining the war.

▲ Passengers in lifeboats watch as the **Lusitania** sinks.

◀ As well as firing torpedoes underwater, U-boats could come to the surface to shoot at enemy ships.

DREADNOUGHTS

The British navy built the HMS *Dreadnought* in 1906. It was a new type of battleship, bigger, faster and stronger than any ships that had been built before. It also carried much bigger guns. More dreadnoughts were built and the Germans started building them too.

▼ The British warship HMS *Dreadnought was the first of many dreadnought ships.*

Communications

Communications in the First World War were very different from those today. Messages were sent by telegraph (written messages sent along wires), telephone and radio. Many communications were sent in code, to stop the enemy from understanding them.

▼ Soldiers releasing a carrier pigeon from a trench.

CODES

Some codes used numbers instead of letters. So if A = 1, B = 2, C =3 and D = 4, then the word BAD would appear as 214. Sometimes letters were switched around, so A = B, B = C, C =D and D = E; then the word BAD would appear as CBE.

▼German officers decoding orders behind the front line in 1914.

CARRIER PIGEONS

Animals such as pigeons and dogs were used to carry messages. Carrier pigeons flew with messages strapped to their legs. Enemy soldiers tried to shoot them or used hawks to catch them. One French pigeon called Cher Ami won the French Croix de Guerre medal for delivering 12 messages during the Battle of Verdun.

▲This machine was used to send coded messages.

Women at war

Before the war, married women were expected to stay at home and care for their families, but some single women had jobs. When the war started, single and married women took over jobs left by men, and filled new jobs made by the war, such as factory work making weapons and shells.

GETTING THE VOTE

The war showed that women were equal to men, but they still weren't given equal rights, such as the right to vote.

At the end of the war, women's demands for the vote grew louder. Some women in Britain and Germany were finally granted the right to vote in 1918; America gave women the right to vote two years later.

▼ *Women working in a munitions factory making shells.*

Edith Cavell

EDITH CAVELL

The British nurse Edith Cavell smuggled more than 200 Allied soldiers out of German-occupied Belgium. In 1915, she was discovered by the Germans and sentenced to death. People around the world were shocked!

Women did not usually take part in the fighting. But in Russia, there was an all-female military unit, called the Battalion of Death!

Artillery shells, machine guns and shrapnel caused dreadful wounds. Many soldiers were killed, some lost limbs, and others were left with mental wounds that would never heal. But as the war went on, huge improvements were made in medical care.

TREATING THE WOUNDED

Wounded soldiers would be carried to a first aid post. Those who were seriously injured were taken to a field hospital, often by horse-drawn ambulances. The field hospitals were about 10 km behind the front line.

▲ *A wounded German soldier on a stretcher. Doctors and stretcher-bearers wore armbands with a red cross, in order to show that they were medics.*

▼ *Many schools and other large houses were turned into hospitals during the war. Here, Indian soldiers rest in a former British palace.*

X-RAYS

During the war, scientist Marie Curie developed mobile X-ray units, which she drove to the front lines. X-rays could show up broken bones, but could also locate bullets stuck inside a wound. Marie Curie won the Nobel Prize for science in 1903 and again in 1911.

Marie Curie

By 1918, only one per cent of wounded soldiers died as a result of their wounds.

BLOOD BANK

Many wounded soldiers needed blood transfusions to replace the blood they had lost. Before the war, blood transfusions were risky, but techniques soon improved. Doctors found a way to stop blood from clotting (sticking in lumps). They also discovered that blood could be refrigerated to make it last longer – this led to the first basic 'blood bank'.

ARTIFICAL LIMBS

Thousands of soldiers lost an arm or a leg in the fighting. The demand for artificial limbs quickly went up. As a result, designs improved and artificial limbs were mass-produced for the first time.

◄ *An artificial arm made during the First World War.*

FACIAL SURGERY

Many soldiers had terrible facial injuries, which made life hard for them back at home. Special hospitals were set up, just for treating facial injuries. Surgeons could reshape men's faces and cover the worst of their scars.

TRIAGE

A new 'triage' system divided the wounded into three groups, so more time could be spent on soldiers who might survive. The groups were:

✚ **Those likely to live, whatever treatment they received.**

✚ **Those likely to die, whatever treatment they received.**

✚ **Those who could be saved only by immediate treatment.**

Home fronts

The war had a huge effect on civilians as well as soldiers. Civilians in France and Belgium suffered the most, as the fighting took place in their towns and cities. Where the German army seized land, they could be hard on the local people. In France and Belgium, 6500 civilians were killed by German forces.

FOOD SHORTAGES

Many countries suffered food shortages. Harvests across Europe had been bad, while enemy ships and U-boats made it hard to import food from abroad. There were food **protests** across Germany, Austria-Hungary and Russia. In many places people died of starvation and illness.

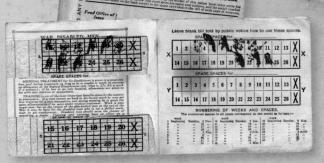

▲ *Whenever someone bought goods, the shopkeeper made a note of the purchase in their ration book. That way, shopkeepers kept track of how much food and petrol each person had bought.*

RATIONING

Rationing was introduced in several countries. The government made sure everyone received the same amount of food, fuel and other products. This meant there was enough to go around.

About 7 million civilians died during the First World War, mostly due to malnutrition and illness.

GOVERNMENT CONTROL

To make sure the maximum effort went into the war, governments took control of farming, railways, mining and factories. Governments also tried to control people's feelings towards the war. There were even laws to stop people from criticizing the war!

PRISON CAMPS

People became increasingly suspicious of foreigners. In some countries, people from abroad were sent to prison camps, in case they were secretly spying on those around them.

▲ *Women and children in Britain queueing in the street for bread.*

1916

The year of big battles

1916 was the year of the bloodiest battles on the Western Front. Each side made a greater effort, throwing more and more men into the fighting. But neither the Allies nor the Central Powers had any great success. It looked like there would be no end to the war.

▲ Reserve soldiers in the French army wait for orders at the Battle of Verdun.

PORTUGAL

SPAIN

ALGERIA

◄ This painting shows French soldiers (those in blue) fighting the Germans at the Battle of Verdun.

KEY EVENTS

21 FEBRUARY – 18 DECEMBER
The Battle of Verdun (see page 38).

9 MARCH
Germany declares war against Portugal.

31 MAY – 1 JUNE
The Battle of Jutland (see page 40).

4 JUNE – 20 SEPTEMBER
The Brusilov Offensive (see page 38).

NORWAY

FINLAND

SWEDEN

DENMARK

North Sea

Baltic Sea

Latvia

Lithuania

UNITED KINGDOM

NETHER-LANDS

Berlin ★

GERMANY

RUSSIA

Poland

Brussels ★
BELGIUM

4

1

FRANCE

SWITZ-ERLAND

AUSTRIA-HUNGARY

2

ROMANIA

Black Sea

ITALY

Corsica
(France)

MONTE-NEGRO

SERBIA

BULGARIA

Sardinia
(Italy)

ALBANIA

GREECE

Aegean
Sea

TURKEY

Sicily
(Italy)

TUNISIA
(France)

Mediterranean Sea

ITALIAN NORTH AFRICA

EGYPT

5

KEY

CENTRAL POWERS
(end of 1916)

ALLIES
(end of 1916)

NEUTRAL NATIONS

Front lines at the
end of 1916

1 Battle of Verdun
(see page 38)

2 Brusilov Offensive
(see page 38)

3 Battle of Jutland
(see page 40)

4 Battle of the Somme
(see pages 42–43)

5 Arab revolt
(see pages 50–51)

0   300 miles

0   500 kilometres

1 JULY – 18 NOVEMBER
The Battle of the Somme (see pages 42–43).

JUNE – DECEMBER
Arab revolt against Turks (see pages 50–51).

28 AUGUST
Italy declares war against Germany (see page 41).

The Battle of Verdun

On 21 February, about 1 million shells were dropped on the French at Verdun.

Germany hoped to knock France out of the war for good – in fact, German General Falkenhayn said he wanted to "bleed France white"! So, on 21 February 1916, the German army launched a massive attack on the French fortress of Verdun. The fighting lasted until December. It was the longest and bloodiest battle of the war.

WHAT HAPPENED?

The battle lasted for months with little change. Then, in June, the Germans nearly broke through the French lines. The French fought them back and bombarded the Germans with heavy attacks for the next six months. In October the French recaptured the area; by December, victory was theirs!

▼ French soldiers shelter during an artillery attack at the Battle of Verdun.

THE BRUSILOV OFFENSIVE

In June, the Russian army planned a surprise attack to divert German troops away from Verdun. On 4 June, the Russian army attacked Austro-Hungarian defences at Lutsk. It was initially a huge success – Russia's greatest in the war – but before long, the Russian army ran out of resources and had to retreat.

THE COST OF VERDUN

The French victory came at a terrible cost. There were 750,000 casualties in total, with 150,000 deaths on each side. France had been bled white, but so had Germany...

Conscription

▲ *This is a group of married British men, who have just been conscripted. Their families have come to wave goodbye.*

At the start of the war, the German, French and Russian armies were largely made up of conscripts – these were men who had to join the army by law when they reached a certain age, usually 18.

WHO WAS CONSCRIPTED?

In Britain the army was mostly made of volunteers. But as the war went on, the army needed more soldiers – fast! The British government introduced **conscription** in 1916. At first, certain groups such as married men and single fathers were excluded, but the rules soon changed.

▶ *This British army poster, featuring Lord Kitchener, encouraged thousands of men to join up.*

"YOUR COUNTRY NEEDS **YOU**"

ALFRED LEETE

BOY SOLDIERS!

Many teenagers were eager to fight – they thought the war would be a great adventure. Thousands of boys lied about their age to join the army. The youngest soldier on record was just 12 years old.

KITCHENER'S PALS BATTALIONS

In Britain, Lord Kitchener decided more men would join up if they did it with their friends. He brought in 'Pals Battalions', formed of men who worked together, lived in one area or played in the same football team.

The Battle of Jutland

Britain and Germany both thought that they had the best navy in the world. Everyone expected there would be a big sea battle between the two navies. This finally took place at Jutland in the North Sea on 31 May 1916.

◄ *A German warship firing at the British fleet during the battle.*

▼ *The Battle of Jutland was the only major naval battle during the First World War.*

WHAT HAPPENED?

German Admiral Reinhard Scheer decided his navy had spent too long in port. He led an expedition to sink British ships in the North Sea – but the British discovered his plan and were ready to meet the German fleet. The fighting lasted a day and a night.

CASUALTIES

The British lost 14 ships, including 3 battle cruisers. The Germans only lost 10 ships and no battle cruisers. The Germans claimed victory, but they never took their fleet back into the North Sea.

The Italian Front

When war was declared in 1914, Italy stayed **neutral** – despite an existing alliance with Germany. Italy said it didn't need to enter the war, because neither Italy nor Germany was under attack. But the Allies wanted Italy to join them...

ITALY JOINS THE WAR

The Allies offered Italy land and money if it would join the war on the Allies' side. On 23 May 1915, Italy declared war on Austria-Hungary. Then, in 1916, it declared war on Germany.

▶ Lots of the Italian army's fighting took place in the high mountains of the Alps.

CAPORETTO

In October 1917, the Italian army looked like it might break Austria-Hungary's defences. But German reinforcements soon arrived and fought back the Italians at the town of Caporetto. The Italians outnumbered the enemy two to one, but they suffered a terrible defeat. Almost 90 per cent of the Italian forces were taken prisoner!

FINAL ITALIAN VICTORY

Despite setbacks, Italy continued to fight off the Austro-Hungarian and German armies. In October 1918, Italy defeated Austria-Hungary's armies in a major battle at Vittorio Veneto.

The Pope hated the war and spoke out against it. Many Italians, who were deeply religious, listened to him and refused to fight.

The Battle of the Somme

The Allies believed a 'Big Push' would break the German lines and win the war. The new commander of the British forces, General Haig, decided on an old-fashioned attack, with **infantry** leading the way, followed by cavalry.

PREPARATIONS

✸ Before the attack, the Allied guns shelled the German lines for seven days and seven nights. They fired nearly 1.6 million shells!

✸ Allied engineers dug deep tunnels under the German front line, and filled them with tonnes of explosives. These went off just before the attack, on 1 July.

INTO BATTLE

At 7.30 am on 1 July 1916, the Allied troops climbed out of their trenches and walked across no man's land towards the German lines. As the Allies marched, the Germans came out of their dug-outs and opened up with machine gun and rifle fire.

▼ *Allied soldiers head across no man's land.*

THE WORST DAY

The first day of the Somme, 1 July 1916, was the worst day in the history of the British army. There were 57,000 **casualties** on this day alone: 19,000 men were killed and 38,000 were wounded.

BARBED WIRE

Both sides used lines of barbed wire to protect their front line trenches. This sharp, spiky wire would trap soldiers climbing over it. Soldiers stuck on the wire made an easy target for gunmen.

BATTLE OF FROMELLES

The Battle of Fromelles (19-20 July 1916) was part of an Allied plan to divert the Germans away from the Somme. Allied troops attacked the town of Fromelles, but the German defences there were very strong. The Allied were defeated with casualties of about 7000, including over 5500 Australian soldiers.

▼ *British soldiers struggle across no man's land during the Battle of the Somme. In the background, a stretcher bearer goes to the aid of a wounded soldier.*

5 MONTHS OF BATTLE

The Battle of the Somme lasted from 1 July 1916 to 18 November 1916. By the end of the battle, over 1 million soldiers were wounded or dead. The Allied forces had only advanced 9.7 km – a distance so small it could be walked in less than 2 hours.

43

Tanks

Tanks were first used by the Allies at the Battle of the Somme. They were armoured vehicles with tracks instead of wheels – this meant that they could move over all sorts of land. Tanks were also armed, either with one big gun or with several machine guns.

DEVELOPING THE TANK

At first, only the British and French had tanks. The Germans didn't develop their own until 1918, near the end of the war.

WATER TANKS

Tanks were developed in Britain in 1915. To keep them top secret, the British called them 'water tanks' – this led to people calling them 'tanks'!

▲ *Tank drivers wore leather and chainmail masks to protect their faces, and especially their eyes.*

▼ *A British Mark IV tank coming over a ridge during training. This model was first used in 1917.*

▼ *This photograph shows a fleet of tanks behind the British lines.*

EARLY TANKS

Early tanks often broke down or got stuck in the muddy ground. Out of 50 tanks that went into the Battle of the Somme, only 9 made it across no man's land to the German lines. But these huge machines were still good at scaring the enemy!

Propaganda

Aeroplanes dropped leaflets over enemy lines, telling soldiers the war was lost and urging them to surrender. Other leaflets said that conditions at home were bad and families were suffering – this was meant to turn soldiers against the war.

Propaganda is information used to shape people's opinions. It was used throughout the war to cheer people up, make them support the war or make them hate the enemy.

◀ *Propaganda told people it was their duty to join the armed forces. This Italian poster says 'Every man must do his duty'.*

▼ *Some posters, such as this US navy poster, made joining the forces look like a fun adventure!*

▲ *This aeroplane is dropping leaflets over France.*

"Fate tutti il vostro dovere!"

PRESTITO CREDITO ITALIAN

JOIN THE NAVY
THE SERVICE FOR FIGHTING MEN
NAVAL RESERVE Wants Unlimited Number of Men RIGHT AWAY
Apply at any Navy Recruiting Office

STRANGE LIES

Most countries lied to the public about how many soldiers had been killed. But some of the lies they told were even stranger. German propaganda spread a story that French doctors were infecting German wells with a terrible disease called the Black Death!

CENSORSHIP

Newspapers had to **censor** material, by cutting out stories that might reveal important secrets. Letters from soldiers to their families were also censored – details of battles or locations were blacked out, in case the letters fell into enemy hands.

1917

The year of change

1917 was the year when things began to change: America entered the war on the side of the Allies and huge changes in Russia led to the country leaving the conflict. Meanwhile, wet weather on the Western Front meant the fighting was bogged down in thick mud.

UNITED KINGDOM

North Sea

London ★

English Channel

NETHER-LANDS

BELGIUM

LUX.

Paris ★

FRANCE

SWITZ-ERLAND

PORTUGAL

SPAIN

Corsica (France)

Balearic Is. (Spain)

Sardinia (Italy)

Mediterranean Sea

ALGERIA

TUNISIA

▼ Mass protests led to two revolutions in Russia.

KEY EVENTS

6 APRIL
The USA declares war on Germany (see page 48).

9–12 APRIL
The Battle of Vimy Ridge (see page 49).

7 JUNE
The Mines of Messines are detonated (see page 53).

31 JULY–6 NOVEMBER
The Battle of Passchendaele (see pages 54–55).

NORWAY
FINLAND
SWEDEN
DENMARK
Baltic Sea
Latvia
Lithuania
Berlin
*
GERMANY
Poland
RUSSIA
Vienna
*
AUSTRIA-
HUNGARY
Ukraine
1
ROMANIA
ITALY
SERBIA
MONTE-
NEGRO
BULGARIA
Black Sea
ALBANIA
Constantinople
*
GREECE
*Aegean
Sea*
TURKEY
Sicily
(Italy)

KEY

	CENTRAL POWERS (end of 1917)
	ALLIES (end of 1917)
	NEUTRAL NATIONS

——— Front lines at the end of 1917

1 Battle of Caporetto (see page 41)

2 Mines of Messines (see page 53)

3 Battle of Passchendaele (see pages 54–55)

4 Russian Revolution (see pages 56–57)

0   300 miles
0   500 kilometres

6 NOVEMBER
The Russian Revolution
(see pages 56–57).

**24 OCTOBER–
12 NOVEMBER**
The Battle of Caporetto
(see page 41).

15 DECEMBER
Fighting stops on
the Eastern Front
(see page 57).

Am rica join– the war

So far, the USA had stayed out of the First World War – the American public saw it as a European conflict, and none of their business. However, the sinking of the *Lusitania* in 1915 had started to change this opinion. In 1917, a German telegram finally brought the USA into the war.

MESSAGE TO MEXICO

Early in 1917, the Germans sent a telegram to Mexico, urging them to go to war with their neighbours, America. The Germans hoped that a conflict so close to home would keep America away from Europe. However, the telegram fell into the hands of the US President, Woodrow Wilson. He was furious at Germany for sending the telegram. On 6 April 1917, the United States of America joined the Allies, and declared war on Germany.

▲ This is the coded telegram sent to Mexico by the German Foreign Secretary in 1917.

Before the war, the US army had 200,000 troops. After the war, it had 2 million!

▲ American soldiers march through New York to mark the United States entering the war.

The Battle of Vimy Ridge

The Vimy Ridge was an area of land that overlooked the town of Arras in France. Its high position gave it good views across the surrounding country, and made it a useful point for defences. The Germans had occupied the Ridge since 1914, but the Allies wanted to take it back!

WHAT HAPPENED?

In April 1917, the Canadian Corps attacked the Vimy Ridge. The attack began at 5.30 a.m. on 9 April. By nightfall on 12 April, the Canadians had taken control of the Ridge, but with heavy losses.

▼ Lorries stuck in the mud on the road near Vimy Ridge in April 1917.

CANADA IN THE WAR

When Britain went to war in 1914, Canada went to war too. Around 620,000 Canadian men and women served in the First World War. The Battle of Vimy Ridge was the first time that all the Canadian Corps fought together. Their impressive victory won the Canadian troops much respect.

▼ Canadian machine gunners take position in shell holes during the Battle of Vimy Ridge.

Th war in th Middle East

The situation in Turkey had hardly changed since 1914. First one side scored success, then the other, but no lasting victories were achieved.

Camels were often used to transport troops in the Middle East.

GAZA

In spring 1917, the British made two attempts to storm the Turkish city of Gaza. In the First Battle of Gaza (March 1917) heavy fog caused confusion – both sides retreated, thinking the other had won! One British general reported that the battle had been a success – so the Allied commanders ordered a second attack. The Second Battle of Gaza (April 1917) lasted three days before the British gave up.

TURKEY

Megiddo ★
Jerusalem ★
Gaza ★
Palestine

BRITISH SUCCESS

In June 1917, the British, led by their new commander General Allenby, launched another attack. Allenby used artillery and cavalry to capture Gaza. Then he attacked the city of Jerusalem. The city surrendered after just two days' fighting.

Many Arabs living inside Turkey were angry with Turkish rulers. Under the leadership of Emir Feisal Ibn Hussein and a British adviser called T. E. Lawrence, they rebelled against the Turkish Empire. Later, they joined the British army to fight against the Turkish.

LAWRENCE OF ARABIA

T. E. Lawrence worked for the British government in Egypt. He believed that the Arabs should have their own state. In 1916, Lawrence joined Arab rebels fighting the Turkish Empire and became one of their leaders.

T . E. Lawrence

◀ Camel ambulances rest in the desert outside Gaza.

▼ British troops pose with guns captured from the Turkish army in Palestine.

ALLIES DEFEAT TURKEY

In September 1918, British and Arab forces attacked the Turkish and German defences at Megiddo in Palestine (an area in the Middle East). By mid-October, the Arabs and the British were in control of the whole area. The Turkish army collapsed and its government surrendered on 30 October.

Prisoner- of war

Men who surrendered to the enemy or were captured in battle were called Prisoners of War (POWs). By the end of the war, there were millions of POWs. Most lived in special camps.

▼ *German soldiers in an Allied Prisoner of War camp in 1917.*

LIFE IN THE CAMPS

Conditions in POW camps were hard, with little food for the prisoners or their captors. In some camps, prisoners were used as slave labour. Many starved to death, or caught deadly illnesses.

PASSING THE TIME

Allied prisoners in German POW camps received the best treatment. Prisoners were allowed to make their own entertainment to pass the time. Some put on plays and concerts for other prisoners.

▼ *A fancy dress party for British and Russian soldiers in a POW camp in Germany.*

THE MINERS

It took six months to dig the tunnels. Most tunnelling was done by men who had worked in mines before the war. It was dangerous work. Exploding shells shook the ground and tunnels sometimes collapsed, burying men alive.

The Mines of Messines

The Allies had spent years trying to capture the Messines Ridge in Belgium. They planned a huge attack for 1917. Before the attack, teams dug 21 tunnels from the British trenches up to the German lines. They were filled with explosives, ready to go off just before the Allies attacked!

▼ *This is one of the huge explosions when the mines were detonated on 7 June 1917.*

THE BIG BANG

When the mines went off on 7 June 1917, the explosion was so huge it was heard in London! About 10,000 German soldiers died straight away. The British and French then pushed forwards. By 14 June, the Allies had taken the Ridge.

455 tonnes of explosives were used. One unexploded mine went off during a thunderstorm in 1955!

Passchendaele

In one place, it took six and a half hours to move a single field gun 230 metres.

54

After success at the Messines Ridge, the Allies pressed ahead. They planned to take the high ground around Passchendaele, near Ypres, which was held by the Germans. The battle that followed is called the Third Battle of Ypres, or the Battle of Passchendaele.

SHELLING THE ENEMY

Before the battle, the Allies fired shells at the German lines for 10 days and 10 nights. But heavy rain flooded craters and turned the land into thick, knee-deep mud.

▲ These Australian troops are studying a giant model of the land around Passchendaele before they go into battle.

▼ *Medics struggle through knee-deep mud with a wounded soldier on a stretcher.*

STUCK IN THE MUD

August 1917 was the wettest August in Belgium for many years. The whole area turned into a muddy swamp. Tanks got stuck in the mud and soldiers could not walk through it. Troops laid wooden walkways, called duckboards, across the mud. Men that fell off could drown in the flooded craters.

OUTCOME

The battle ended when Canadian forces captured Passchendaele on 6 November. The Battle of Passchendaele gained the Allies just 8 km of land, but there were about a quarter of a million casualties on both sides.

▼ *Canadian soldiers carry wooden duckboards across the muddy landscape of Passchendaele.*

The Russian Revolution

At the start of the war, Russia was ruled by an emperor, called the Tsar, and his wife, the Tsarina. Their family had a rich lifestyle, but life was hard for ordinary Russians. Failure in the war, food shortages and money problems had made people unhappy and angry.

▲ Tsar Nicholas and his family pose for a portrait. Following the Russian Revolution in 1917, the Russian royal family were executed by Bolsheviks in 1918.

FEBRUARY REVOLUTION

On 8 March 1917, women marched into Petrograd (now St. Petersburg) demanding bread. When the march turned into an angry protest, the Tsarina called in soldiers to control the crowds – but many soldiers joined in with the protest instead! Workers and soldiers set up their own government and forced the Tsar to abdicate (give up the throne).

Vladimir Ilyich Lenin

OCTOBER REVOLUTION

After the Tsar gave up the throne, a new government took over. The war against the Central Powers continued – but it was not going well. Meanwhile, many people the Tsar had banished came back to Russia. One of them was Vladimir Ilyich Lenin.

Lenin was a revolutionary – meaning he wanted to change the way that Russia was run. He was the leader of a group called the Bolsheviks, who seized power in Russia in November 1917. They went on to set up a **communist** state.

▼ Lenin was a great public speaker. In this painting, he is shown giving a speech at a Bolshevik party meeting.

▶ This Russian poster calls people to join the revolution.

PEACE TALKS

The war had been going badly for Russia for some time. The new Bolshevik government decided to withdraw from the war. In December, they met with the Central Powers and agreed to stop fighting on the Eastern Front.

In 1918, a Spanish flu epidemic killed more people worldwide than the whole war!

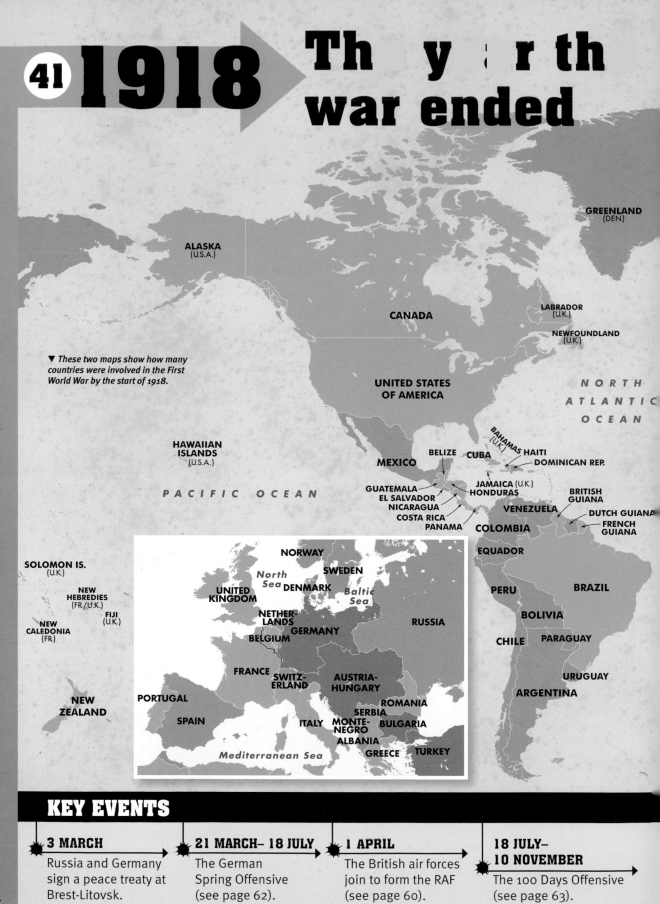

▼ These two maps show how many countries were involved in the First World War by the start of 1918.

GREENLAND (DEN)

ALASKA (U.S.A.)

CANADA

LABRADOR (U.K.)

NEWFOUNDLAND (U.K.)

UNITED STATES OF AMERICA

NORTH ATLANTIC OCEAN

HAWAIIAN ISLANDS (U.S.A.)

BAHAMAS (U.K.)

MEXICO

BELIZE CUBA HAITI

DOMINICAN REP.

JAMAICA (U.K.)

PACIFIC OCEAN

GUATEMALA
EL SALVADOR
NICARAGUA
COSTA RICA
PANAMA

HONDURAS

VENEZUELA

BRITISH GUIANA

DUTCH GUIANA

FRENCH GUIANA

COLOMBIA

EQUADOR

SOLOMON IS. (U.K.)

NEW HEBREDIES (FR./U.K.)

FIJI (U.K.)

NEW CALEDONIA (FR.)

PERU

BRAZIL

BOLIVIA

PARAGUAY

CHILE

NEW ZEALAND

NORWAY

SWEDEN

North Sea

DENMARK

Baltic Sea

UNITED KINGDOM

NETHER-LANDS

GERMANY

RUSSIA

BELGIUM

FRANCE

SWITZ-ERLAND

AUSTRIA-HUNGARY

PORTUGAL

SPAIN

ITALY

SERBIA

MONTE-NEGRO

ALBANIA

ROMANIA

BULGARIA

GREECE

TURKEY

Mediterranean Sea

URUGUAY

ARGENTINA

KEY EVENTS

3 MARCH
Russia and Germany sign a peace treaty at Brest-Litovsk.

21 MARCH– 18 JULY
The German Spring Offensive (see page 62).

1 APRIL
The British air forces join to form the RAF (see page 60).

18 JULY–10 NOVEMBER
The 100 Days Offensive (see page 63).

By 1918, both armies were exhausted. But several big attacks were about to bring the war to an end. On 11 November 1918, the Central Powers and the Allies signed an agreement to end the war.

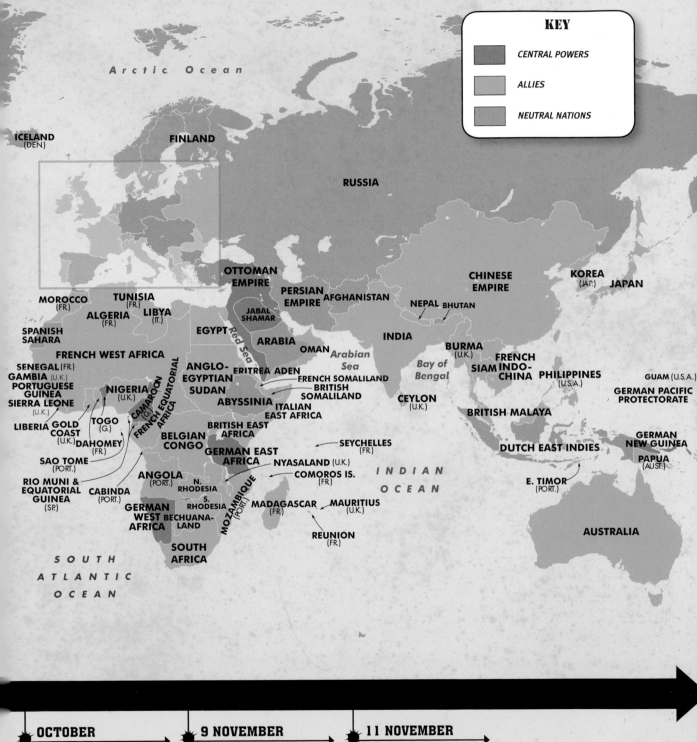

KEY

CENTRAL POWERS

ALLIES

NEUTRAL NATIONS

Arctic Ocean

ICELAND (DEN)

FINLAND

RUSSIA

MOROCCO (FR.)

TUNISIA (FR.)

ALGERIA (FR.)

LIBYA (IT.)

OTTOMAN EMPIRE

PERSIAN EMPIRE

AFGHANISTAN

CHINESE EMPIRE

KOREA (JAP.)

JAPAN

SPANISH SAHARA

EGYPT

JABAL SHAMAR

ARABIA

OMAN

Arabian Sea

INDIA

NEPAL

BHUTAN

FRENCH WEST AFRICA

Red Sea

ERITREA

ADEN

FRENCH SOMALILAND

Bay of Bengal

BURMA (U.K.)

FRENCH INDO-CHINA

PHILIPPINES (U.S.A.)

GUAM (U.S.A.)

SENEGAL (FR.)

GAMBIA (U.K.)

PORTUGUESE GUINEA

SIERRA LEONE (U.K.)

LIBERIA

NIGERIA (U.K.)

ANGLO-EGYPTIAN SUDAN

BRITISH SOMALILAND

SIAM

GERMAN PACIFIC PROTECTORATE

CAMEROON (G.)

FRENCH EQUATORIAL AFRICA

ABYSSINIA

ITALIAN EAST AFRICA

CEYLON (U.K.)

BRITISH MALAYA

TOGO (G.)

GOLD COAST (U.K.)

DAHOMEY (FR.)

BELGIAN CONGO

BRITISH EAST AFRICA

DUTCH EAST INDIES

GERMAN NEW GUINEA

SAO TOME (PORT.)

GERMAN EAST AFRICA

SEYCHELLES (FR)

INDIAN OCEAN

PAPUA (AUST.)

RIO MUNI & EQUATORIAL GUINEA (SP.)

CABINDA (PORT.)

ANGOLA (PORT.)

N. RHODESIA

NYASALAND (U.K.)

COMOROS IS. (FR.)

E. TIMOR (PORT.)

GERMAN WEST AFRICA

BECHUANA-LAND

S. RHODESIA

MOZAMBIQUE (PORT.)

MADAGASCAR (FR.)

MAURITIUS (U.K.)

AUSTRALIA

SOUTH AFRICA

REUNION (FR.)

SOUTH ATLANTIC OCEAN

OCTOBER
The German mutiny (see page 64).

9 NOVEMBER
The German Kaiser abdicates (see page 64).

11 NOVEMBER
The Armistice is signed to end the war (see page 65).

War in the skies

Both sides used aircraft from the start of the war. Early on, planes were used to watch the enemy from the skies and find out how many men and guns they had. As the war went on, aircraft designs changed and enemy aircraft started to fight each other in the skies.

LEADING THE WAY

The French were the leaders in developing aeroplanes. At the start of the war, the French Air Force was the biggest on the Western Front. Many American pilots flew in the French Air Force before America joined the war in 1917.

▶ German Fokker D7 and Fokker tri-planes (aeroplanes with three pairs of wings) pursue a group of British DH7 aeroplanes.

An American airman shooting at enemy aircraft.

GUNS ON PLANES

At first, planes were not equipped with guns. If enemy aircraft met, the pilots would shoot at each other with pistols. Before long, machine guns were added – but they fired at the propeller and sometimes brought down their own plane! In 1915, designs changed to make sure this couldn't happen.

DANGER!

Flying planes in the First World War was very dangerous. The planes were flimsy constructions made from wood and cloth. If a bullet hit the fuel tank the plane would catch fire. Most pilots did not even have parachutes, so they couldn't bail out!

THE RED BARON

The most successful fighter pilot in the war was the German Manfred von Richthofen – also called the Red Baron because of his red plane. He shot down 80 Allied planes during the war.

Manfred von Richthofen

GOTHA RAID ON LONDON

The Gotha was a large German biplane (an aeroplane with two pairs of wings), with a wingspan of 24 metres. It was designed for long-range bombing raids. Through 1917 and 1918, Gotha bombed London, Paris and other Allied cities.

▼ German Gotha planes had two pairs of wings and two engines.

The Spring Offensive

In Spring 1918, the Allies were failing but the Americans were on their way. The Germans decided to launch a surprise attack to defeat the Allies before US support could arrive. They hoped this would end the war for good.

TOO FAST

In March, Germany launched major attacks along the Western Front. They were very successful and the Germans advanced quickly. But the speed of their advance exhausted them. Food supplies and artillery could not keep up, and the soldiers had to carry all of their own supplies.

STORMTROOPERS

During the offensive, the Germans used a specialist group of soldiers known as the 'stormtroopers'. They were fast, well-trained and heavily armed. Stormtroopers slipped through the enemy lines to attack them from the side and the rear.

▼ *Masked German Stormtroopers advance through a wood as part of the Spring Offensive.*

▲ *French and English soldiers fighting alongside each other at the Marne in 1918.*

LAST EFFORT

The Allies launched a series of counter-attacks. On 28 May, the Americans launched their first offensive of the war and forced the Germans to retreat. Allied defences stopped the Germans' final offensive at the Marne in June.

The Hundred Days Offensive

As the Central Powers were struggling, the Allies struck back. This started a final series of battles fought over 100 days.

▼ Allied soldiers rest on the banks of the St Quentin Canal after storming the Hindenburg Line. The canal had been an important part of the Line.

THE HINDENBURG LINE

The Hindenburg Line was a series of fortifications built by the Germans in 1916. It was 140 km long and up to 5 km wide. Each section had concrete barriers, trenches, barbed wire and machine-gun posts. The Germans believed no one could break through the Line.

BREAKING THE LINE

In September, the Allies started bombarding the Line with gunfire, while tanks and soldiers closed in. By the end of the month, the Allies had broken through the Line. From then on, the German army was in full retreat.

The German mutiny

In October, senior officers in the German navy planned an attack on Britain. Many sailors thought it would be a suicide mission, so they refused to go. Sailors across Germany stopped following orders. It was a **mutiny!**

MUTINY SPREADS

Soldiers and civilians across Germany were angry and felt that the war had been lost. When they heard about the naval mutiny, people in factories and army bases joined in too.

▼ *Revolutionary sailors at a port in Hamburg, Germany, in 1918.*

PEACE TALKS

In October, officials from Germany and Austria-Hungary approached the Allies to discuss ending the war. On 3 November, Austria-Hungary signed an armistice with the Allies. But Germany would not agree to peace.

THE KAISER FLEES

By early November, the German Kaiser realized the war was lost. He signed an order putting the German Chancellor, Prince Max von Baden, in charge of Germany. Then, on 9 November 1918, he gave up the throne and fled Germany.

The Armistice

On 11 November 1918, German and Allied leaders met in a railway carriage in woods near the Western Front. There they signed an **armistice**, agreeing to stop the fighting. The guns finally stopped at 11 a.m. that day.

▲ The German and Allied leaders meet on a train to sign the Armistice and end the war.

CELEBRATIONS

▼ Soldiers celebrate as the armistice is announced.

When the war ended, huge celebrations took place all over the world. Millions of people threw street parties with decorations, food, dancing and games. The Allies arranged parades and firework displays to celebrate their victory.

By the end of the war, over 100 countries around the world had been involved.

The Treaty of Versailles

After the war, the nations involved met at the Palace of Versailles, outside Paris. There, on 28 June 1919, they signed a treaty to agree the terms of peace.

As early as January 1918, President Wilson had made a peace plan that would be fair to everyone. Some of the points included: reducing the size of armies; giving people control to rule themselves; freeing the colonies and starting the League of Nations.

GERMANY'S TERMS

Many people wanted to make Germany pay for starting the war. Germany had to agree to the following terms:

☑ Germany lost 13.5 per cent of its territory (including 7 million people)

☑ Germany lost all of its overseas territories

☑ Germany had to pay £6.6 billion to the Allies

☑ Any union between Germany and Austria-Hungary was forbidden

☑ The German army was limited to 100,000 men

☑ Military conscription was banned

☑ Big guns, tanks, aircraft and submarines were banned

▼ Signatures on the Treaty of Versailles

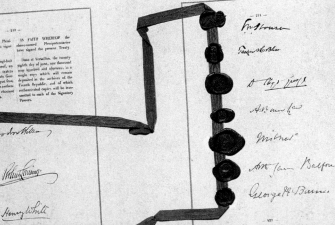

LEAGUE OF NATIONS

The League of Nations was a group of representatives from around the world. Their aim was to settle disagreements between countries so that war could be avoided. However, the French refused to let the Central Powers join. The newly formed Soviet Union (Russia) also refused to join.

Four more treaties were made with the Central Powers after the Treaty of Versailles.

▼ *Crowds gather outside the Palace of Versailles as the treaty is signed.*

British Prime Minister Lloyd George, French President Clemenceau and US President Wilson led the Allied leaders at the peace meetings that followed the war. They were nicknamed 'the big three'.

David Lloyd George

Georges Clemenceau

Woodrow Wilson

48 The lost generation

Throughout the war, around 65 million men from around the world joined up to fight. Around 9 million of them died – many of those under the age of 30. So many young men died that they are sometimes called 'the lost generation'.

A man who lost both of his hands in the war uses prosthetic (artificial) hands to work on a farm.

LIFE AFTER THE WAR

Of the men who survived, many had physical or mental disabilities. By the end of the war, many thousands of soldiers had lost an arm or a leg. Many soldiers were blinded, or suffered illnesses for the rest of their lives because of poison gas attacks.

SHELL-SHOCK

The stresses of war gave many soldiers an illness called 'shell-shock'. It affected men in different ways: some had terrible nightmares; some lost the ability to move or speak; others couldn't stop shaking. Today this is called 'combat stress', but at the time it was misunderstood. Many men with shell-shock were called cowards.

◄ Two men who lost the use of their arms learn to do work using their mouths.

◄ A wounded soldier learns to walk again on prosthetic legs.

▼ Soldiers with shell-shock take up gardening to help them recover.

CIVILIAN DEATHS

As well as military deaths, there were millions of civilian deaths during the war. Some civilians were killed by invading soldiers or bombing attacks, but many more died from disease or famine brought about by the war.

CASUALTIES

✝ **ALLIED CASUALTIES**
Dead: 5,712,379
Wounded: 12,809,280

✝ **CENTRAL POWER CASUALTIES**
Dead: 4,010,241
Wounded: 8,419,533

After the war

For those involved in the war, things would never be the same again. Russia had overthrown its royal family and become a communist country: Soviet Russia. Germany had also lost its royal family, and was heavily in **debt**. The death of so many men and the huge cost of the war affected people right around the world.

▼ *Over four years of battle had reduced much of Europe to rubble and mud. This photograph of Ypres, taken in 1919, shows how the city was flattened by the war.*

THE EMPIRES

The war put an end to the Turkish, Russian, German and Austro-Hungarian empires. But it also threatened other empires. Many colonial countries had fought in the war and felt they had won the right to their independence.

POWER FOR WOMEN

During the war years, women had shown they could do the work of men. After the war, many countries finally gave women the right to vote and the right to work.

French suffragettes protesting for their right to vote.

UNHAPPY GERMANY

Some politicians thought Germany would react badly if it were punished after the war. They were soon proved right... Just 10 years after the First World War, Germany's **economy** was in a mess. A new leader, the former soldier Adolf Hitler, rose to power. In 1939 he led Germany into another world war.

▲ *A young Adolf Hitler in German First World War uniform.*

AMERICA AFTER THE WAR

The war was a turning point for America's economy. By the end of the war, the USA had taken over much of the manufacturing formerly done in France and Britain. It had also benefitted from loaning money to European countries. It was set to become the most powerful country in the world.

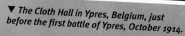

▼ *The Cloth Hall in Ypres, Belgium, just before the first battle of Ypres, October 1914.*

Remembering the fallen

Nations around the world still remember the millions of people who died during the First World War. Special ceremonies of remembrance are held around war memorials or in religious buildings. In most places, Remembrance Day is held on the date of the Armistice, at 11 a.m. on 11 November.

MEMORIALS

In most cities, towns and villages across Europe, North America, India and Australasia there are memorials to those who died in the first and second world wars. The names go on and on – lists of friends, brothers and fathers who went to fight and never came home.

THE UNKNOWN SOLDIER

Many soldiers could not be identified after they died and lots of bodies were lost in the mud of the Western Front. In some countries there is a special tomb for the 'unknown soldier' – one unidentified soldier who represents all the others.

▼ The grave of the unknown soldier in Westminster Abbey, London.

▼ Huge cemeteries stretch across parts of France and Belgium, where most of the fighting on the Western Front took place. This cemetery is in Verdun, France.

SYMBOLS OF REMEMBRANCE

In Britain and Canada, people wear poppies as a symbol of remembrance. The poppy was chosen because so many of them grew across the fields of Flanders in Belgium. At first the poppies were made by disabled ex-servicemen in order to raise money. Other nations have different symbols of remembrance, for example the Bleuet de France.

▲ British and Canadian poppy of remembrance

▶ Bleuet de France, the French symbol of remembrance.

ANZAC DAY

In Australia and New Zealand, the most important date in the remembrance calendar is 25 April – Anzac Day. This remembers those Australians and New Zealanders (Anzacs) who died during the world wars, particularly the many who died in the Gallipoli campaign of 1915.

WHO'S WHO?
The Allies

The Allies were led by Britain, France, Russia and America (after 1917). The other Allied countries were Belgium, nations in the British and French Empires, Italy, Japan, Romania, Greece, Brazil and Siam (now Thailand). There was also some support from Portugal and China. Here are some of the most important political and military figures in the Allies:

Herbert Asquith

British Prime Minister: 1914–1916
Asquith led Britain into war in 1914. After the Battle of the Somme, he was blamed for military failures and replaced.

David Lloyd George

British Prime Minister: 1916–1922
British War Minister: 1916–1918
When Asquith resigned in 1916, Lloyd George became Prime Minister of a new government.

Sir John French

British Commander in Chief: 1914–1915
French was 66 when he was given command of British forces. He was replaced by Haig in 1915.

Sir Douglas Haig

British Field Marshal (head of the British forces): 1916–1918
Haig replaced Sir John French as head of the British forces. He retired in 1919.

Field Marshal Horatio Earl Kitchener

British War Minister: 1914–1916
Kitchener was Britain's most distinguished soldier. He died in 1916 when his ship hit a floating mine.

Admiral Sir John Jellicoe

Commander in Chief of Britain's Grand Fleet: 1914–1916
Jellicoe was in command of the British Fleet during the Battle of Jutland in 1916.

Georges Clemenceau

Prime Minister of France: 1917–1920
Clemenceau helped to establish Ferdinand Foch as leader of the Allied forces.

Marshal Joseph Joffre

Head of French Forces: 1914–1916
Joffre is most famous for leading the Allied armies at the Battle of the Marne. After Verdun, he was replaced by Nivelle.

General Robert Nivelle

French Commander in Chief: 1916–1917
Nivelle became a French hero after the Battle of Verdun in 1916.

General Henri-Phillipe Petain

French Commander-in-Chief: 1917–1918
Petain took command when there were mutinies in the French army. He helped to restore order.

Marshal Ferdinand Foch

Commander-in-Chief of all the Allied Armies: March 1918–November 1918
Foch was the first person to control all of the Allied forces in France.

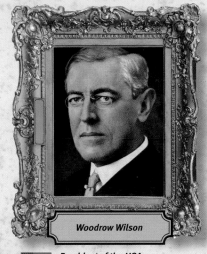

Woodrow Wilson

President of the USA: 1913–1921
Wilson brought the United States of America into the First World War in 1917.

General John Pershing

Commander of American forces: 1917–1924
Pershing brought the US army from 500,000 men in 1917 to nearly 3 million in 1918.

Tsar Nicholas II

Emperor of Russia and Russian Head of State: 1894–1917
Nicholas II was the last Russian tsar. He was overthrown in 1917 and executed in 1918.

Duke Nicholas Nikolaevich

Commander in Chief of the Russian army: 1914–1915
Nikolaevich was the uncle of Tsar Nicholas II.

WHO'S WHO?
The Central Powers

The Central Powers consisted of Germany, Austria-Hungary, Turkey (the Ottoman Empire) and Bulgaria. Here are some of the most important political and military figures in the Central Powers:

Kaiser Wilhelm II

King of Prussia and Emperor of Germany: 1888–1918
Although Kaiser Wilhelm was Commander in Chief he had little say in military decisions.

Field Marshal Helmuth von Moltke

Chief of the German General Staff: 1906–1914
Doubts about Moltke's decision-making led to him being replaced by Falkenhayn in 1914.

General Erich von Falkenhayn

Chief of the German General Staff: 1914–1916
After the German defeat at Verdun, Falkenhayn was replaced by Hindenberg.

Paul von Beneckendorf und von Hindenberg

German Chief of Staff: 1916–1918
Hindenberg was Germany's most famous soldier. He was 67 when the war started.

General Erich von Ludendorff

German First Quartermaster General: 1916–1918
Luddendorff was the un-credited power behind the German military.

Franz Josef I

Emperor of Austria-Hungary and Commander in Chief: 1848–1916
When Josef I died in 1916, his grandnephew became Emperor Karl I.

Karl I

Emperor of Austria-Hungary:
1916–1918
Karl I left politics in 1918 when Austria decided not to have a royal family.

Istvan Tisza

Prime Minister of Hungary:
1913–1918
Istvan Tisza was assassinated in 1918 and replaced by Móric Esterházy.

Field Marshal Franz Conrad von Hotzendorf

Hungarian Chief of General Staff:
1912–1918
After several military failures, Conrad was dismissed by the new Emperor in 1917.

General Arthur Arz von Straussenberg

Commander in Chief of the Austro-Hungarian army: 1917–1918
Straussenberg quickly rose through the army ranks. He was a key advisor to Emperor Karl I.

Ferdinand I

Tsar of Bulgaria:
1908–1918
In 1918, the Allies forced Ferdinand to give up his throne to his son Boris III.

Vasil Radoslavov

Bulgarian Prime Minister:
1913–1918
Radoslavov was one of Ferdinand I's greatest advisors during the war.

Nikolai Zhekov

Commander in Chief of the Bulgarian army: 1915–1918
Tsar Ferdinand refused to be Commander in Chief and appointed Zhekov instead.

Mehmed V

Sultan:
1909–1918
Mehmed V was Sultan of the Ottoman Empire but he had little real power.

Enver Pasha

Turkish Minister of War:
1914–1918
Turkish army officer who became Ruler of Turkey and Commander in Chief in his 30s.

GLOSSARY

ALLIANCE
A partnership between countries.

ARMISTICE
An agreement between countries to stop fighting.

ARTILLERY
Guns of all sizes, from pistols up to the very biggest guns, called field guns.

ASSASSINATE
To kill someone important for political reasons.

BLOCKADE
To stop movement in or out of a place, for instance by placing ships in front of a harbour to stop other ships from leaving or entering it.

CASUALTIES
People that were killed or wounded in battle.

CEASEFIRE
When both sides in a war agree to stop fighting. This can be temporary, or permanent.

CENSORSHIP
When newspapers, radio and other media are banned from revealing certain information. This can be to hide an important secret or to cover up something that the government disapproves of.

CIVILIANS
People who are not members of the armed forces.

COLONY
A country that is governed by another country, often a long way away.

COMMUNIST
A person who believes that there should be no rich or poor in society, but that everyone should share money and possessions equally.

CONSCRIPTION
Government laws that force people to join the armed forces.

DEBT
Someone who is in debt owes money to somebody else.

ECONOMY
The financial state of a country. In a healthy economy, a country has lots of money to share among its people.

FRONT
The place on a battlefield where two armies fight one another.

HOME FRONT
Day to day life of ordinary people at home, when their country is at war.

INFANTRY
Soldiers in an army who fight on foot.

LOAN
To lend someone money.

MUTINY
When people rise up in protest against their leaders, for example when soldiers or sailors refuse to obey commands.

NEUTRAL
A neutral country is one that does not take sides, or take part, in a war.

PROPAGANDA
Information and stories that are used to make people believe something. They are often exaggerated or untrue.

PROTEST
To complain about something. Mass protest is when lots of people that are unhappy about a certain thing gather together.

RATION
To share goods out in set-sized portions. Rationing is used when there is a shortage of food or other goods.

REBELLION
When a lot of people rise up in angry protest at their leaders.

RETREAT
When an army is losing a battle and goes backwards to escape the enemy.

REVOLUTION
A rebellion where the people want to get rid of their leaders and replace them with other people.

SHELL
A rocket-shaped bomb that is fired from a very big gun.

SHRAPNEL
Sharp pieces of metal that fly out when a bomb explodes.

SNIPER
A soldier who can hit a target a long way away, using a long-barrelled gun called a rifle. Snipers often shoot from a hiding place.

SURRENDER
When soldiers put up their hands, put down their weapons and give up to the enemy.

TORPEDO
A long, pointed weapon, fired underwater from a submarine to destroy other submarines or ships.

TREATY
An agreement between countries after a war is over.

INDEX

Picture credits (t=top, b=bottom, l=left, r=right, c=centre, fc=front cover)

Maps by: Meridian Mapping
Alamy: 5t, 67br, 74bl, 74br, 75br, 75bc, 76bc Classic Image; 5c Lordprice Collection; 5b Heritage Image Partnership Ltd; 18, 19c Mary Evans Picture Library; 19b, 30t, 51r, 71b, 75tc The Art Archive; 23c The Keasbury-Gordon Photograph Archive; 26t Photos 12; 28–29 akg-images; 34–35 GL Archive; 39r, 75cc Pictorial Press Ltd; 40t, 52 INTERFOTO; 67tr, 67ct, 74tl, 74tc, 75cl Archive Pics; 72b Neil McAllister; 74tr Peter Stone – Archive; 74bc Image Asset Management Ltd; 75tr The Print Collecto; 75cr North Wind Picture Archives; 75bc Chris Hellier; 76 bl Ivy Close Images; 77br The Keasbury-Gordon Photograph Archive
Corbis: fcr 91040/united archives/dpa; bc, 8, 12c, 12b, 17, 27, 32b, 60b Bettmann; 5 adoc-photos; 28 Hulton-Deutsch Collection; 41 Paul Thompson/National Geographic Society; 60–61 Derek Bayes Aspect/Lebrecht Music & Arts; 72–73 Tim Graham; 64, 68t, 68–69 Berliner Verlag/Archiv/dpa
Dorling Kindersley: bct, bcbl, Gary Ombler
Dreamstime: fcc, fcl Samvaughan67
Getty Images: 6, 11c, 13r, 14–15, 30c, 32–33, 32t, 36t, 39t, 40c, 50–51, 56t, 65, 68–69, 70b, 71t; fc Lambert; fc, 31c Roger Viollet; bc Richard Caton II Woodville; fc, 44b, 48c, 54b UIG via Getty Images; 13c Popperfoto; 16c, 44, 55t, 63 IWM via Getty Images; 20b 2013 Getty; 26c Dorling Kindersley; 26b SSPL via Getty Images; 29t De Agostini; 29b Time & Life Pictures; 33t, 44t SSPL via Getty Images; 34b Linda Steward; 36b Roger Viollet; 45l Time & Life Pictures; 56–57 DEA PICTURE LIBRARY, 57b DEA / G. DAGLI ORTI; 62, 66–67, 70–71 Popperfoto
Library and Archives Canada: 54–55 William Rider-Rider / Canada. Ministère de la défense nationale / Bibliothèque et Archives Canada / PA-002084
Mary Evans Picture Library: 51b, 65t, 75tr; 4 INTERFOTO / Sammlung Rauch; fc, 10, 11r, 15t, 15b, 16b, 24, 49c, 53c Robert Hunt Collection; 76tr, 76br Robert Hunt Library; 18b SZ Photo / Scherl; 22c Sueddeutsche Zeitung Photo; 23b Pump Park Photography; 25c Robert Hunt Collection/ Imperial War Museum; 31 GROSVENOR PRINTS; 38 SZ Photo / Scherl; 42–43, 48t The Everett Collection; 43t, 52b, 69t, 77cc Illustrated London News Ltd; 46b Interfoto; 57t Epic/PVDE; 61b Imperial War Museum/Robert Hunt Library; 62b Epic/Tallandier; 76tl, 76tc PHILIP TALMAGE; 77tl Imagno; 77tc SZ Photo / Knorr + Hirth; 77tr SZ Photo / Scherl; 77cr Sueddeutsche Zeitung Photo; 77bc Grenville Collins Postcard Collection
Shutterstock: fcc, 25c Zsolt Horvath; fc, 73t Jane Rix; fcb Gary Blakeley; fcc stephen mulcahey; bc Darq; fc Olemac; fctr Kletr; fctl Mettus; fct Sergey Kamshylin; bc, fc Pavel L Photo and Video; bccl kylesmith; fcb Olemac; fctr igor.stevanovic; bcr Horst Kanzek; bcbr Oleg_Mit; fc Kushch Dmitry; fc TonLammerts; fc Vaughan Sam; fc, 30l Ensuper; bc fotorobs; fc alexsvirid; bc a katz; fc zimand; fc Gavran333; fc Gary Blakeley; fc Zerbor; fc Archiwiz; fc IanC66; fc sharpnerl bc zimand; fc Fer Gregory; 5r, 31r, 32b, 61t, 67r, 74–77 Iakov Filimonov; 25, 31 Lack-O'Keen; 35b, 53tl Jeremy; 41b DeCe; 53b Vector; 71t VoodooDot
The Advertising Archives: 45c, 45r Images Courtesy of The Advertising Archives
Wikimedia Commons: 37t Claude TRUONG-NGOC; 77 cl, 77bl public domain